LOCAL HISTORY: A GUIDE FOR RESEARCH AND WRITING

James Mahoney

National Education Association
Washington, D.C.

Copyright © 1981
National Education Association of the United States

Stock No. 1682-3-00

Note
The opinions expressed in this publication should not be construed as representing the policy or position of the National Education Association. Materials published as part of the Analysis and Action Series are intended to be discussion documents for teachers who are concerned with specialized interests of the profession.

Library of Congress Cataloging in Publication Data

Mahoney, James.
  Local history.

  (Analysis and action series)
  Bibliography: p.
  1. Local history. 2. Historical research.
I. Title. II. Series.
D13.M25   907'.2   80-26231
ISBN 0-8106-1682-3

I hear and I forget,
I see and I remember,
I do and I understand.

—Chinese Proverb

The Author
James Mahoney, a former classroom teacher, is now an elementary school principal in the Maysville Local School District, South Zanesville, Ohio.

The Advisory Panel
Benjamin M. Hughes, teacher, Red Bluff Union High School, Red Bluff, California

Helen Fretic Lawler, Counselor and former Social Studies Team Leader, Marple Newtown Junior High School, Newtown, Pennsylvania

Joyce Smith, Associate Professor of Education, Georgia College, Milledgeville

Manerva D. Todd, social studies teacher, Normandy Senior High School, Saint Louis County, Missouri

James Wilson, U.S. History teacher, Hampton High School, Virginia

CONTENTS

PREFACE 7

CHAPTER 1
INTRODUCING LOCAL HISTORY 8

CHAPTER 2
STARTING THE PROJECT 11
    Setting the Goals—Selecting the Topics—Determining the Specific Area and Scope—

CHAPTER 3
RESEARCHING LOCAL HISTORY 20
    Libraries—Historical Societies—Public Records—School Records—Business Records—Church Records—Newspapers and Periodicals—Personal Papers—Physical Remains—Cemeteries and Genealogy—Maps, Atlases, Gazeteers—Pictures and Photographs—Oral History—Summary—

CHAPTER 4
ORGANIZING AND EVALUATING THE RESEARCH 36
    Research Guidelines—Organizing the Material—Interpreting and Evaluating the Material—

CHAPTER 5
WRITING AND PUBLISHING LOCAL HISTORY 39
    Components of the Book—Preparing the Dummy—Selecting a Printer—Financing the Project—

CHAPTER 6
STUDENT PARTICIPATION 44

CHAPTER 7
LOCAL HISTORY ACTIVITIES 47
  Slide-Tape Presentations—Archaeological Digs—Dramatics—Genealogy—Visiting Cemeteries—Communicative Education—History Fairs—Bulletin Boards—Historical Geography—Time Capsules—Junior Historical Society—Field Trips—

APPENDIX A
OUTLINE FOR RESEARCHING AND WRITING LOCAL HISTORY 53

APPENDIX B
INTERVIEW SHEET 60

APPENDIX C
KEY SHEET FOR TRANSCRIBING ORAL TAPES 62

RECOMMENDED READINGS 63

PREFACE

This project really began in the fall of 1974 when my seventh graders began asking some local history questions for which I had no answers. After promising to look into the matter, I researched several libraries and found no works written exclusively about Lawrence Township. The students and I decided then to do our own research on the subject.

During the first months we collected the available written information about Lawrence Township, exhausting the local sources—township records, letters, old newspapers, diaries, and church records. As we gathered each item and shared it with the class, a good framework for a book began to emerge.

The most exciting part of the project came in the summer of 1975 when we started interviewing many residents of the community, people who were especially cooperative. With two students accompanying me at each interview, we recorded questions and answers on tape.

Then in June 1976 my eighth grade published *The Wilderness That Became Lawrence*. It was an amazing success. A community of less than six hundred people bought eight hundred copies of the 156-page book in three weeks.

This guide is an outgrowth of that project. Its purpose is to provide teachers and other interested persons the necessary know-how to undertake such a project. It is our story. Although in a sense it remains unfinished today, I have still used our local history in conducting many class activities.

It is my hope that many more local histories will be written. Projects of this type can be one of the most exciting motivational tools ever devised to enhance the learning and understanding of history for both upper elementary and secondary students.

This guide is therefore about kids—whose effort, enthusiasm, and hard work brought it about. To them, the students of Lawrence School, I shall always be grateful.

Finally, I would like to thank Claude Davis for his suggestions and editing, Robert Miller for many hours of editing, and Diana Gearhart for typing the manuscript.

CHAPTER 1
INTRODUCING LOCAL HISTORY

Local history is a narrative of people and of the communities in which they lived. Generally, it is a very small geographic unit of study, focusing on ordinary people and their significance. Because history too often is regarded as the study of only famous people and events, the attraction of local history is that it is very personalized. It is the story of one's own community—what happened there, why it happened, when it happened, and who made it happen. For effective use in upper elementary and secondary schools, however, local history should not be treated as a separate entity. It should be integrated into the history curriculum. Indeed, it is a part of the state and national history.

> And doing it yourself, you find out a great deal about American History, about the great transformation from a transcontinental wilderness into the world's most powerful nation; from a primitive subsistence economy into one producing the world's highest standard of living; from a colonial monarchy (part French, part English, part Spanish) into a democracy where every individual, through the ballot and freedom of speech, assembly, and petition, has the right to a voice in his government; from a rather rigid society structured on European models into a highly fluid society in which a man can in general rise according to his ability. You discern this easily and dramatically because you see how it happened (and who made it happen) right in your own community.[1]

Thus, local history is a microscopic approach to the study of United States history. As one undertakes its study, parallels will emerge between the two. For example, just as our national history is filled with exciting dramas and great leaders, so is local history.

Probably the teacher's most natural question before undertaking such a project is Why study local history?

> Local history can be tied in with national history; indeed there is no subject that does not have its parallel in the local scene. Early pioneer life, the development of industrialization, political campaigns, social issues, and countless other subjects are mirrored in the history of almost every village, town, city, county, or state. Once students see that history is all about them, their interest is unlimited.[2]

Indeed, it does motivate students. It takes them from the stage of listening about history to "doing it." (See chapter 6, "Student Participation.") By embarking upon a local history project, students' enthusiasm will grow with each new discovery about themselves and their community. Many will develop an interest in history. Local history encourages inductive and deductive thinking by testing generalizations of the national scene against the local one and vice versa.[3] Teachers can use it for instructional strategies. The illustrative materials enhance and enrich the study of United States history. In short, local history personalizes an often impersonal subject. Thus, its study is readily justifiable educationally. Another aspect is its impact upon residents of the community. For example, as our project began to take shape and grow, the amount of community attention it received was amazing. Moreover, student enthusiasm increased in proportion to that of the community.

This book gives a step-by-step account of the many learning situations we encountered in our project. As Eliot Wigginton, the teacher whose students prepared *The Foxfire Book,* observed in his introduction to that work:

> ... English, in its simplest definition, is communication—reaching out and touching people with words, sounds, and visual images.... In their work with photography (which must tell the story with as much impact and clarity as the words), text (which must be grammatically correct except in the use of pure dialect from tapes that they transcribe), layout, makeup, correspondence, art and cover design, and selection of manuscripts from outside poets and writers—to say nothing of related skills such as fund raising, typing, retailing, advertising, and speaking at conferences and public meetings—[students] learn more about English than from any other curriculum I could devise. Moreover, this curriculum has built-in motivations and immediate tangible rewards.[4]

A local history project takes on the same aspects of communication described by Wigginton. Thus, as students begin to identify and work with the local community's past, they leave behind the traditional American history classroom setting.

When undertaking a local history, the first aspect to consider is the approach. There are several possible routes to follow: (1) epochal—selecting a specific time period or era in the community's story, especially one of great impact; (2) topical—choosing a particular area of interest; (3) narrative—involving a chronological review of important events; and (4) biographical—concentrating on various persons who, in some way, influenced the community. The choice of a suitable approach will help avoid the mere accumulation of a group of unrelated facts.

Several variables will shape the approach once it is chosen. First is the geographical unit to be studied. If it is large in terms of population, it may be well to limit the project to a particular topic such as education, religion, or folklore.

The second variable is any unique aspect of the community. Perhaps an important national event took place there—the town or area was the site of a great oil boom or gold rush—or an important national figure lived there. If so, it may be well to concentrate on that event or person. Whatever the community's area of uniqueness, it should make an excellent topic for a local history.

The third variable that will shape the approach is the material already written about the community. A trip to the local library should answer this question. If something has been done, can it be added to? Don't feel discouraged if it turns out that a great deal has been written about the community. There will be some topic not yet covered.

The fourth variable to consider is the interest of students. Perhaps a certain topic or era is especially appealing and interesting to them. If so, this is a logical approach to begin with.

Finally, to a large degree the most important variable will be the availability of historical sources. In the beginning stages of the work, it may be necessary to alter the approach in light of these sources.

Local history projects can be one of the most exciting and useful methods of instruction ever devised. Indeed, the only limitations are the imagination and creativity of teacher and students. Whether the area to be investigated is urban or rural, however, the variables remain the same.

Regardless of scope and approach, the end product of the project (book, pamphlet, article) may become a stepping stone to other useful purposes. A book of local history can become a supplementary history text, for example. It should also be noted that the end product need not be something in written form; the historical process may lead to several different types of activities such as audiovisual presentations. In fact, many followup activities can result from the project. These and others which may be carried out during the various stages of the research are discussed in a subsequent chapter.

REFERENCES

[1] Francis P. Weisenburger, *Ohio: A Student's Guide to Localized History* (New York: Columbia University, Teachers College Press, 1965), p. v.

[2] Ralph Adams Brown and William G. Tyrell, "How to Use Local History," How to Do It Series, No. 3 (Washington, D.C.: National Council for the Social Studies, 1961), p. 1.

[3]Daniel Van Leuvan, "Local History Aids the Teaching of American History," *Social Studies* 62 (November 1971): 247–48.

[4]Eliot Wigginton, ed., *The Foxfire Book* (Garden City, N.Y.: Anchor Press, Doubleday, 1972), p. 13.

CHAPTER 2
STARTING THE PROJECT

Setting the Goals

As often quoted, "The longest journey begins with a single step." Selecting the topic(s) for the local history project can be a very difficult task. Before starting, one must ask some basic questions. The first question, "What is this project trying to do?" adds direction for the amateur historian and leads to goal setting. For example, a classroom teacher may respond that the class's purpose is to research a localized area of history. Closely related is a second question, "What is the point of this project?" The point may simply be to stimulate students' interest in history by encouraging active involvement in the historical process in their own area. And finally, "What do we hope to accomplish?" The answer to this can be stated in terms of a behavioral objective: "As a result of our project, students will be able to research public records."

These responses will provide the teacher with some general direction for the project. The questioning is thus important for focusing attention on the objectives. It may also be true that the goals can change in light of the variables, discussed in the previous chapter, which tend to affect and shape the project.

Selecting the Topics

After setting the goals, it is time to decide upon an area of local history to study. There are two different approaches to this selection: (1) choosing topics from a general outline of local history elements and (2) brainstorming areas of local interest. A discussion of both methods follows. It should be clear that regardless of the method chosen, the result will be to set one "on track" before researching the project.

General Outline

I found Donald Parker's *Local History: How to Gather It, Write It, and Publish It* an excellent resource for anyone interested in local history for any reason. Parker provides an outline for researching and writing local history which is extremely helpful in selecting topics. The outline (reprinted in Appendix A) gives a very comprehensive view of the elements of local history, as indicated in the following skeleton:

    I. Geography and Topography
    II. Antiquities—Indians
    III. Pioneer Settlement
    IV. Economic Developments
    V. Political Activities
    VI. Religious Developments
    VII. Population History
    VIII. The Family
    IX. Education
    X. Newspapers, Periodicals, and Libraries
    XI. Social and Fraternal Organizations
    XII. Other Cultural Activities: The Arts
    XIII. Science and Technology
    XIV. Law
    XV. Social Problems and Reform
    XVI. Recreation
    XVII. Folklore[1]

These basic topical areas are useful to start a local history investigation. Parker then breaks down each general topic into specialized areas of inquiry within the topic. No doubt some of the topics included will not be applicable in some situations. For example, there may be no information available on certain subjects or there may not be time to explore others. Perhaps one topic had a great impact on the community. If so, it may be advisable to limit the study to this. Or if the class is especially interested in studying certain phases of a topic, these may be the best areas to concentrate on. Whatever the particular situation may be, teachers must determine the most feasible and appropriate topic(s) of study for their students.

Brainstorming

The second approach to selecting the topic(s) for study, is a well-devised teaching tool for promoting student imagination and creativity. In brainstorming, the teacher introduces a topic or question and encourages students to think up as many ideas as possible. The keynote to this method is quantity. All ideas are considered acceptable and written on the chalkboard. From this quantity will come the quality of ideas desired.

Brainstorming local history involves a free and open consideration and discussion of all ideas. To stimulate this activity in the classroom, the teacher may initiate ideas in several ways. One method is to find material already written about the local area and present it to the class orally or in written form. Usually students will find it interesting to discuss hometown matters because the information is very personalized. Questions that may arise from this type of material are unlimited. For example, the teacher may ask students if they had any relatives in a particular relevant event. Following the open discussion of various topics, it is logical to proceed with the question "What doesn't this article or oral report tell us?" This is a way to select ideas based on student interest and inquiries. Indeed, it opens Pandora's box for further discussion, and also establishes the basis for the project, namely, the topic(s).

Another way for the teacher to stimulate such a brainstorming session is to relate national history to local history. For example, if a class is studying the Civil War in American history, it is very easy to shift the focus of an event to the local scene.

The teacher can also initiate local history brainstorming by asking leading questions such as "If our history textbook were on local history, what would the chapters be about?" Or "If we were to teach others about our local history, what could we tell them?" Questions of this nature tend to bring out student knowledge of their community's past. In addition, they point out student interests in their local history.

In my own experience, the brainstorming method was particularly effective in the classroom. Student response was enthusiastic and the discussion was very productive. In answer to the query "What questions can we ask about our local area?" typical replies included the following: "Who were the first settlers here? Why did they come?" "When was this school built? Where was the first school? What subjects were taught?"

"Did geography affect the settlement of this area?" "When did they start the volunteer fire department?" "What kinds of jobs did people have in earlier days?" "Who were some of the heroes of our community?" "How did our township get its name?" "Were there any churches which aren't here any longer?" Literally hundreds of ideas and questions can arise from this type of discussion. After I listed the comments on the chalkboard, the class searched for a way of organizing them. In this manner, the essence of inductive-deductive reasoning, the class arrived at the following generalized topics:

    I. Government
   II. Education
  III. Early History and Settlement
  IV. Local Organizations
   V. Economic Development
  VI. Religion
 VII. Folklore
VIII. Personalities
  IX. Contemporary Community
   X. Geography
  XI. Unusual Circumstances
 XII. Miscellaneous

Then we spent more time focusing on what each section required and devised a rough outline in each category as follows:

  I. Government
    A. Early form of local government
    B. Early political leaders
    C. General operation
    D. Present form of local government

This brief outline of government gave some focus and direction to student efforts. Through their own method, my students determined what they should investigate in this area. Much of what they wrote about township government came from records of proceedings they researched. Students pored over pages of minutes from the post-Civil War era to the present day. In addition, they talked to township officials about the role of local government in the community today. Other classes, of course, may add many more elements to this topic. It is important to keep in mind, however, that an outline may grow larger or smaller in light of specific research.

    II. Education
        A. Early schools
           1. Location
           2. Teachers
           3. Curriculum—subjects taught
           4. Extracurricular activities
           5. Transportation
           6. Financing
        B. Organization changes and consolidations
        C. Present organization and administrators

Education has undergone many changes from the one-room schoolhouse to the large consolidated school. Because it tends to be the one common experience for all people of a local community, most of whom remember their schooldays, information on this topic is relatively easy to obtain and verify. Most students find it a particularly appealing subject to investigate. My class spent many hours researching board of education meetings as well as interviewing retired school employees to discover how things had changed in the schools. Students especially enjoyed stories of how teachers used to "keep school."

    III. Early History and Settlement
        A. The first settlers
           1. Motivation for immigration
           2. Character sketches
           3. Hardships
           4. Settling steps
        B. Role of Indians
        C. Famous events

The idea here was to gain an understanding of the background of the early settlers and the problems they faced. Earlier histories of the area can be particularly revealing. Often they contain character sketches of the more colorful local personalities. In addition, the community may have been the site of an event of historical significance. As a result of their research, my students discovered that the first children's home in the state of Ohio was established in our township.

IV. Local Organizations
   A. Types
   B. Functions
   C. Leaders
   D. Relation to the community

In this area students identified and explored civic or non-civic-related groups that had an impact on the community. The topic may include the development of a volunteer fire department, for example, which can be easily traced through newspaper accounts and/or minutes of meetings kept by such volunteer organizations. It may also include groups that have disappeared from the local scene after making some contribution.

V. Economic Development
   A. Role of natural resources
   B. Effect of location
   C. Agriculture
      1. Main crops
      2. Farming methods and implements
      3. Livestock
   D. Manufacturing
      1. Early industries
      2. Local resources for industry
      3. Occupations

Depending on the local area, this category may be broadened extensively to include the role of labor unions, maritime activities, and other economic activities that may have affected the community. Here, especially, it is important to devise categories according to the uniqueness of the particular area. For my own class, an oil boom greatly influenced the community. Therefore interest centered upon that aspect of economic development. We found that at the time of the oil boom thousands converged upon one area of our township. As further evidence of this economic boom, a resident offered the class several old pictures of the areas showing the tremendous temporary growth.

VI. Religion
   A. Early churches and denominations
   B. Effect on social and moral life
   C. Contemporary churches

Religious groups tend to exert a great deal of influence in many communities. The real task here was to determine the effect of religion upon the lives of the people. From church records my students explored the history of each church in the township. As members of the various congregations, they were extremely interested in gathering this information. It included detailed accounts written by many clergymen about the problems they faced, many providing an interpretation of the period. For example, "Whiskey was the motive for power, both for men and boys . . . accidents were common. . . . I found slavery and intemperance my most formidable foe."

    VII. Folklore
        A. Superstitions
        B. Stories passed down
        C. Name derivations

This category may have some fascinating avenues to explore. Nothing tends to stir the minds of creative students so much as local myths surrounding certain structures, or good ghost stories. Another area to investigate is the origin of local geographical names. In this area, perhaps more than in any other, my class heard many interesting stories. One story, for example, concerned a creek in the central part of the township which originates in a nearby community mentioned in early county histories as Morse Run. Both the creek and the community took their name from a local manufacturer. According to the story told by a retired teacher, the name was changed to its present form—Moss Run—because the community of Morse Run was a station on the Underground Railroad during the pre-Civil War period. It became well known among the slaves escaping by the railroad, and their southern dialect changed the pronunciation to "Moss Run," and this name stuck.

    VIII. Personalities
        A. Famous and infamous
        B. Most remembered

In this category students focus on the people who have had an impact upon the community. Indeed, one approach to the study of local history is to research and prepare biographical sketches of the famous and enduring personalities of the area. For example, my students were interested in learning about a woman who served as the administrative head of the township schools for over 30 years. They heard many stories of her dedication, concern, and often fiery temper. The students also discovered that the township high school had the first female coach of a boys' varsity basketball team in the state of Ohio during World War II. Now retired and living in a nearby community, the former coach gave the class a picture of the team and provided interesting accounts of her coaching style.

    IX. Contemporary Community
        A. Major occupations
        B. Private businesses or corporations
        C. Recreational facilities

This category can serve as a valuable historical reference for the future; its aim is to describe life as it is lived today. This is probably the easiest topic to research because the people and records are readily available. In researching the contemporary community, however, one is inevitably drawn to the past. For example, the current owner of a general store in our township, located in the community of Dart, was able to share with my class information about the history of the store and its previous owners from the nineteenth century to date. He also told us the story behind the community name. In 1905, during a discussion of a name for the post office, several birds "darted by." Hence the name.

    X. Geography
        A. General landscape
        B. Natural resources
        C. Climate
        D. General effect upon the community

In many regions, geographical conditions have played a major role in the settlement of the area. Some settlements began near an important body of water or mineral resource. Given a particular location, the settlement evolves with certain social and economic results. After studying township maps, my students wrote essays and discussed reasons for the settlements in our area.

    XI. Unusual Circumstances
        A. Natural disasters
        B. Major crimes or scandals
        C. Tragedies

This area can provide ideas for researchers who wish to explore spectacular headline events of their local history. In some cases, the nature of a particular event or tragedy can influence the very structure of the community. Often these events may be heartbreaking, but residents cannot forget them. For example, because our township is intersected by the Little Muskingum River, it has experienced three major floods in its history. Townspeople supplied stories and pictures of the resulting devastation in the community for our local history project.

I do not recommend a task of such enormity for the beginner. My students spent nearly two years researching these topics because the scope of the project was so extensive.

Determining the Specific Area and Scope

The two approaches that have been described provide for a free discussion of ideas and categories leading to the selection of topics. With an assemblage of possible topics for research, teacher and students are ready to move to the next step of the process—"What does one do with these subjects of local history?" The answer to this question determines the specific area and scope of the project. Several options are available to the class. Obviously, one is to limit the study to a single area—for example, the history of education in the community or some striking event such as the big oil boom of 1880. Or time may be an important factor to consider. It would be foolish to investigate a community's entire history in one year. I was fortunate enough to have the same students every day for two years, a situation that allowed a much more extensive study. Whatever the scope of the topic(s), consider the amount of time available for conducting the project.

Another option is to have different classes take separate areas to study. At the end, each class can compile its work. In a small school, a self-contained class can compile and write on a topic for the year. After several years the different sections from several classes can be compiled. In larger schools, of course, several classes can work on different subjects at the same time. It is especially helpful to gain the cooperation of other teachers in such cases. For example, an English instructor might take a class to investigate religion in the community; a history class might study education. Then, at the end, the work of the various groups can be combined.

Still another possibility is the individual or small team term project, with each person assuming responsibility to research a single topic or part of a topic.

Again, a reminder that although this discussion concerns a final product in written form, alternatives to a written local history exist and are discussed later in this book (see chapter 7). In addition, the scope and subjects of the project originally chosen may very well change in light of data found as the research progresses.

At this point, when the goals of the project have been set, the topics chosen, and the scope determined, student enthusiasm should be high. Now it is time to take history from the realm of discussion to that of action. The next step is probably the most exciting of all—researching. Like detectives, students are about to find clues and answers to the questions posed. Many unanticipated discoveries will come forth. If there is one thing to be learned from research, it is to expect the unexpected. The class is ready to start on its adventure!

REFERENCE

1. Donald Dean Parker, *Local History: How to Gather It, Write It, and Publish It* (New York: Social Science Research Council, 1944), p. 103.

CHAPTER 3
RESEARCHING LOCAL HISTORY

Research, the real thrust of any local history project, can also be the most exciting part. It is the careful investigation of facts about the area under examination. Historical sources of information fall into two categories: primary (original) and secondary. Primary sources are first-hand records or accounts. Although they are usually more accurate than secondary sources, they may be more difficult to evaluate. Secondary sources are often a more finished product derived directly from primary sources. However, one must exercise caution in using secondary sources, for they may include a biased interpretation of the original facts. For example, in researching education in a local area, a primary source of information would be past board of education records of proceedings. After examining these minutes, the researcher would make conclusions about educational decisions made, money spent, and so forth. Suppose, however, someone had already completed such an investigation and written about it. This work would represent a secondary source. Upon comparing the two sources, the researcher might well find some of the conclusions and interpretations of the secondary source different from her/his own. In such instances, when additional secondary sources are available, it may be advisable to consult several of these. Regardless of the source that may be used, however, the information needs to be organized and evaluated. Chapter 4 suggests guidelines for this process, as well as for note-taking. The purpose of this chapter is to provide the reader with information on the sources of local history.

Libraries

The first step should be a visit to the local library, where the librarian will probably be the most important resource person for the project. In most cases, material about the local area will be available because a large number of county histories (of varying caliber) were written in the late nineteenth century. Many of these publications were commercial ventures which required people to pay for their inclusion in the work. They can, however, be a valuable source of local information. For example, in studying a township I found a county history published in 1888 which contained only a very short section on the township. One paragraph mentioned that the first children's home in Ohio had begun in the locality. This was a tremendous revelation, as the fact was not commonly known in the community and it gave the class a particularly dramatic event to pursue. The county history thus helped focus the study.

If there is nothing in writing about the local area, do not be discouraged. The lack of a history may provide the motivation and enthusiasm for students to do one of their own.

After the first stop at the local library, the complete and written information gathered there should provide ideas for further research. The following pages discuss the remaining sources, together with information on where to find them and how best to use them.

Historical Societies

There are many local, regional, and state historical societies. Each has genealogical and historical research materials available for use, although the type and quantity may differ from one organization to another. Most state historical societies have library facilities which, for a small charge, will usually supply the information available in their records on a particular person. The important sources to be found in these collections include federal census returns, military rosters, published family histories, genealogical periodicals, newspapers, maps, atlases, and directories. Researchers can use the materials according to need. In many cases, the officers and members of the associations are also very helpful in providing information. Oftentimes, these people have private collections of material which they are willing to share.

Public Records

Public records are particularly useful in investigating local government. Most townships are governed by a board of trustees which can provide all the past records of proceedings. Before researching the records of any organizational body, however, it is important to know how the group functioned; otherwise it is difficult to understand its records. Therefore it can be very helpful if, before going through the township records, part of the class meets with the trustees for an explanation of their operations. Then, these records can be very informative.

Receipts and disbursements of public funds over the years give an indication of the cost of government. In addition, various ordinances enacted in the past can offer an idea of the kind of problems the community experienced during a particular period. For example, the type of punishment specified for certain crimes can provide information concerning what early citizens considered "serious offenses." Certain laws still on the books may also afford some surprises—such as the Trenton, New Jersey, ordinance forbidding sheepherders to wear false faces while driving their charges through town, or the Kentucky law holding a person negligent who walks behind a mule without speaking to the animal.[1]

> There are around 81,000 units of local government with assorted names, duties, and structures within the fifty states. Not all of them keep their records permanently, or keep records historians are likely to need. The most reliable clues for the researchers must be based on practices within a given state.[2]

Some of the more common public records—not all found at the local level—include land transactions, vital statistics, judicial records, tax records, marriage records, title deeds, census records, local laws, and military records. Depending on the area and intensity of the investigation, it may be necessary to use some or all of these materials. For most purposes, however, local township records are sufficient.

School Records

These records are necessary for any basic investigation of local education. In my own case, I found board of education proceedings going back to 1924, when the township's one-room schools were first consolidated. Laboriously, the class went through all the minutes, which were found in the present board of education office. From these records, the class was able to identify the many personnel employed during this time. In addition, policies passed by previous boards showed many changes over the years.

Students particularly enjoy researching yearbooks, another type of school record. These publications not only offer many pictures of interest, but they provide accurate accounts of athletic records and outstanding school functions.

Business Records

> Not only do business records show the local historian what has taken place, but through the use of such records he can follow the relations of business and government; trace the rise of credit institutions; . . . and give the history of labor.[3]

Business records can range from those of very large companies to those of small general stores. They may be hard to find, however, since owners of businesses often change and records may be lost or destroyed. Small family businesses are more likely to have useful records, especially if they have been established for many years. Such records are valuable for learning about the buying habits of people during particular time periods based on the items they purchased. Price comparisons can also prove very revealing. Overall, these records provide a picture of the local economy.

Church Records

Another obvious field of investigation is the religion of an area. Not only do church records prove valuable in this respect, but they can also provide information about local issues and feelings at particular times. Many local churches have very old and well-kept records, although the information and organization of each set may differ widely. All church records, however, should contain information on membership, births, deaths, marriages, and expenses.

What proved most valuable to my students were notes made by various ministers. Several were written in diary fashion, noting the curious happenings of the time. One of the more interesting accounts came from one minister's memoirs written in 1843 about the people, living in log cabins, who were motivated by whiskey power:

> I found slavery and intemperance my most formidable foes. . . . There was now great work to be done, to combat irreligion, skepticism,

and unconditional salvation which in many parts of this region then prevailed.

The author further related a story of an attack by a plantation owner in Virginia (now West Virginia, across the Ohio River from his home) who accused him of stealing slaves.[4] This record was a good example of a historic source illustrating a wide range of local opinions and feelings.

Newspapers and Periodicals

In their simplest sense, newspapers are diaries of a particular community, mirroring the daily life of the people. A word of caution may be necessary, however, when using them as a research source. As Thomas Felt notes, newspaper publishing is a business enterprise. Advertising therefore plays an important financial role. Thus, "As a reflection of community life and attitudes, newspapers tend to be limited by the tolerance of advertising."[5] This caution is not meant to downgrade the importance of newspapers as a historical source—they can provide a wealth of information—but it should be kept in mind.

Many librarians have local periodicals on microfilm. The newspaper office may also have similar records. In my own community the major newspaper, which has all its back issues on microfilm, going back to the middle of the nineteenth century, permitted the class to use the microfilm and scanner at the office.

Since newspapers serve a wide area, they are useful for checking various events learned about elsewhere. Scanning a local journal may be easier and faster than scanning all the old files in other sources, because so little of its contents may deal directly with the community. For example, my class learned from the county history that a large oil well had been discovered on school property in 1870. Using this information, students found a much more detailed description in old newspaper accounts. A similar use of the newspaper came when students were substantiating information from another source that a local citizen had been the U.S. Ambassador to Russia during World War I. A student who wrote the State Department inquiring about the man received a reply giving the dates he served as ambassador as well as information that he died in a local hospital in 1945. As a result, students found an obituary on microfilm with a wealth of information about the man who previously was known only as a former ambassador.

Newspaper advertising can provide data on the type of goods sold and the prices charged during any given time period. Newspapers and periodicals published in an area also afford an excellent insight into the various attitudes and issues of the day. If time is limited, an alternative use of these publications is to prepare a random sampling to read for ideas, pictures, etc.

Personal Papers

Personal papers, consisting of diaries, family letters, notes, memos, scrapbooks, can provide very vivid and rich accounts of life in a community. For obvious reasons usually they are not readily available. However, this may not be the case once a local history project becomes known to the members of the community. A surprising number of people may come forth with such materials once they are aware of a class project.

It is important to involve students as researchers in the discovery of these materials. In my class, for example, the great-aunt of one student had taught forty years at the school and had kept an accurate account of many important events that occurred during her lifetime. In addition, she had compiled stories told her as a young woman by community members who had long since died. When she heard what the class was doing, the sister of the teacher gave all of her personal papers to the student. These papers proved to be a rich source of information, helping establish dates and providing many character sketches of earlier residents.

This is only one example of finding and using personal papers; others were forthcoming as our research continued. There is a little of the detective in everyone, it seems—students not excepted. When motivated, they will dig up diaries and many other old personal papers. And in addition to adding to the class research, they will discover many interesting things about their families' past. One student came to class one morning with an old paper saying, "Hey, Mr. Mahoney, I found out my great-great-great-grandfather fought in the Civil War and we found his discharge papers." Needless to say when studying the Civil War that year, the student's interest was unparalleled.

Again, many of these materials will be forthcoming as the class's enthusiasm rubs off on the entire community. Oftentimes leads such as "Mr. Smith is supposed to have . . ." will turn up. Make it a point to contact such individuals. In many cases, these leads will pay great dividends in terms of new information discovered. Also, remember to obtain permission to use any information found in personal papers.

Physical Remains

Physical remains consist of virtually everything that would be left if people were to disappear from the earth. One could easily write a history about the many structures in a community, accompanied by fascinating stories telling why they were built, who built them, and what their use was. The physical remains that my class researched were old items owned by local residents that were brought to our attention. For example, one elderly resident of the community had an antiquated mowing machine. On a visit to his farm, students took pictures of the machine and taped an explanation of its original use. This is one method of researching physical remains. Because this source is almost unlimited, however, a decision should be made whether such items will fit into the scope of the project.

Another example of the use of this source came from an old newspaper article about Lewis Wetzell, a famous frontier scout during the Revolutionary War period who spent a great deal of time in our township. The article described a cave Wetzell used to hide in and gave its location. One Saturday morning shortly after reading the article, several students hiked to find the cave. They found it high above the Little Muskingum River and were fascinated by the view it offered—a perfect place to hide for observing activity on the river. The students took several pictures of the cave—one the view of the Little Muskingum River which later became the cover of our local history book. Such material serves to add to student enthusiasm.

Another type of physical remains is architecture. Building design and style may provide ideas on the town's development.

Cemeteries and Genealogy

Visiting cemeteries can supply the class with a method of date verification as well as an interesting experience. This research point comes later when students know more about the people of the community. Hunting the tombstones of the early settlers of the area can be exciting. Epitaphs often include odd or amusing inscriptions such as the following which was used for advertising by an early local citizen:

> Here lies Jane Smith, wife of Thomas Smith, Marble Cutter. This monument was erected by her husband as a tribute to her memory and a specimen of his handiwork. Monuments of this style are two hundred and fifty dollars.

Another of a more amusing nature found by a researcher read:

> Underneath this pile of stones lies all that's left of Sally Jones. Her name was Lord, it was not Jones, but Jones was used to rhyme with stones.

While such epitaphs may not offer a wealth of information, they do serve as interest-maintaining devices. Other inscriptions, however, may provide information on the manner in which death came to many people—such as a great flood or epidemic in a certain year.

And, of course, students may use tombstones to establish facts about their own genealogy. Visits to cemeteries often lead to the discovery of missing names and dates of students' relatives. At the start of the project, have each person start a family tree. In addition to helping students discover their past, the information they find can often help the entire class in the research process. A final note—the more the class activities relate to students' personal lives, the more student interest and enthusiasm will be maintained.

Maps, Atlases, Gazeteers

Maps and atlases can assist in determining the effect of the physical landscape on the community's settlement and livelihood. Atlases in particular often contain historical statements of value. The county engineer's office should have a basic map of the area, which can aid in locating unfamiliar places. Although in many cases early maps may be just sketches of the area, they can be extremely informative when compared to current maps. Map interpretation by students can supply varied insights into the community over a period of time.

An excellent source of historical data, gazeteers are of a different nature from maps and atlases. Formerly called emigrant directories or pocket registers, they are geographical dictionaries or indexes. They are of immense value in fixing local names and providing details of travel routes, commodity prices, and fare rates. They are often found in the collection of the historical society.[6] Gazeteers may also indicate name changes in certain places. Discovering the reasons for such changes can provide numerous examples of local folklore. Particularly in rural settings, many roads were commonly known by names not given officially on maps. In such instances, students might make a map to include in the project.

Pictures and Photographs

A good picture is indeed worth a thousand words! If there's one thing most people enjoy, it's looking at old photographs. The local history project should include many. Beyond the fact of enjoyment, however, photographs serve as an important historical source of information—they are records of the way people lived. Quite a few of the photographs students collect will be of remains that no longer exist; therefore they can sometimes help settle location arguments.

Picture collections can come from a number of sources—private citizens, historical societies, churches, schools, newspapers. Usually, local institutions are especially generous in lending photographs and granting permission for their use. In addition to such collections, students may take pictures of their own for a special section on the contemporary community. This part of the project should give interested people in the future a good historical perspective of the present period.

Pictures can also provide a great source of expressiveness that may be lacking in a literary sense. Furthermore, by comparing and contrasting photographs, students can gain a sense of humility and appreciation—as they view the community's situation as they know it in the present against what it was in the past.

Every local history project will benefit from making pictures an integral part of the search into the past. A final note—remember not only to take especially good care of pictures on loan, but to obtain the owner's permission to reproduce those to be used in the project.

Oral History

Most simply, this source consists of individuals relating their experiences, descriptions, reminiscences, or accounts of general or specific events of the past. Recorded for future use, the oral interview is a means of facilitating the accumulation of historical material. It is not extremely technical or expensive. In our project, the only expense was for tapes (which can be financed by fund-raising activities such as school bake sales).

The historian's role has many facets, involving research, explanation, and interpretation of sources. To accomplish these tasks, the historian utilizes the tools available—written texts, primary and secondary sources, records, and many other materials such as those described in the preceding sections. Those who do a local history, of course, use many of the same sources. But the most important tool in the local project may be oral history. Historians are constantly seeking the role of motivation in their study of the past. Given a set of facts, they tend to speculate on the *why*—in terms of modern scholarship or what they believe the mood of the period to have been. This is a necessity, because in most cases they were not there on the scene. Oral history can lend great insight into the why of many past occurrences, because the people who are interviewed have often lived the events that are to be interpreted. Thus they can clarify the facts that are known and add color and detail to them.

For most purposes, recorded interviews with citizens of the local area are indispensable. These tapes have many logical advantages and applications. First, the recorded information supplies a vast wealth of data not obtainable elsewhere. The interviewee helps one collect knowledge of the past.

Second, the people interviewed may add much detail to those events about which something is already known. For example, from public records my students knew that the first high school was built in 1925 in the central part of the township. They could have accepted that fact and let it stand alone. When interviewing a citizen, however, they found out not only who donated the land, who the teachers were, and what subjects were taught, but also that later another building was rented behind the school and a telephone line planted between the two buildings for communication. Oral history provides many similar examples of a simple fact being built upon and becoming a story itself.

Third, education needs the support of the public. Students and teachers going out into the community to collect information can bring the school and the public together. People are glad to help, especially many of the senior citizens. Although not necessarily an aim of the project and/or the interview, a successful public relations program may be an unexpected result.

Finally, and most important from personal observation, is the effect of these activities on students. History suddenly becomes interesting. The grandfather of one of my students was the leading scorer on the township's first basketball team. The great-great-grandfather of another won a medal at Shiloh, and, suddenly, that student wanted to know more about the Civil War. Local history was a microcosm of our country's history. But now, students felt a part of that history because their ancestors were participants. They began to realize that history is not just famous places, names, and dates to be memorized, but the study of everyone's past. And they began to realize that everyone's forebears played a part in our heritage. Indeed, they experienced an emergence of pride in their past. Perhaps one student said it best in an evaluation of our project when she wrote, "... Even though a certain area is very small, it can still become a very important part of someone's life." Another wrote, "A place full of good people, with kind hearts. A place where people can be proud of who and where they are."

Methodology of Oral History

Perhaps most important, at least for future classes, was the methodology I arrived at in doing oral history. In fact, much of it was trial and error. Most historians who conduct oral histories tend to use one of two approaches: autobiographical or topical. The final solution may be a mixture of both. In the autobiographical method, the interviewer encourages the interviewee to speak freely of his/her experiences. The advantage is that the person may disclose information the interviewer may not have thought to ask. It also takes pressure off the interviewee to give the "right" answer. From its very structure, however, this method can lead to "rambling on."[7] Another disadvantage is that many people prefer to be asked questions, to know what is expected of them.

The second major method for conducting oral history is the topical approach. Here, the interviewee is limited to certain topics, which helps avoid rambling on and irrelevancies.[8] However, this approach requires more homework on the part of the questioner who must know what to ask. But it can be extremely useful in interviewing people for specific details. For example, in researching the origin and organization of a township's volunteer fire department, armed with a previously compiled list of questions, an interviewer of a charter member can do well.

This leads to a third approach, one designed after conducting interviews according to the two preceding methods. Because the autobiographical method may work well with one person and the topical method with another, it may be difficult to determine the appropriate method until the interview is over. To help eliminate this problem, it is necessary to know what information is desired from any individual. This, of course, requires some knowledge about the individual before the interview. Obviously, a retired teacher in the township might provide great insight into early education in the township, but probably little concerning the organization of the Grange unless the teacher were a member. What is needed, then, is some sort of interview instrument, or a written outline to be used during an interview. The instrument should be designed flexibly enough to encompass the advantages of the autobiographical approach yet rigidly enough to keep to the desired topics, thus avoiding irrelevancies. Before designing such an instrument it is necessary to decide the areas of the community to be explored. Through discussion my class arrived at the following categories:

Early History and Settlement
Education

Government
Religion
Geography
Economic Development
Organizations
Contemporary Community
Miscellaneous
Folklore
Unusual Circumstances

Once we completed these topics, our purpose was to investigate, research, and explore them to their fullest and then write about them. How easy it all seemed! By brainstorming the various categories, we designed an interview sheet (see Appendix B). Students received copies of the sheet, together with an explanation for its use. With such an instrument as a guideline the interviewee was able to describe in autobiographical fashion the specific topics of interest to the researcher. From my personal observation, the instrument worked beautifully. Some organization and order are necessary to do the tapes. The chief value of any instrument is that it allows the persons recorded to expound on those subjects with which they are most familiar and to simply pass over those with which they are least familiar. The interview sheet gives the direction needed to conduct the interviews. Further, the use of this method makes subsequent transcription of the tapes much easier and more intelligible.

Certainly before any interview, the interviewer will have a good idea of the interviewee's area(s) of expertise, but this instrument can catch many errors or omissions. For example, one would not expect a retired teacher to be extremely knowledgeable about farming. A purely topical approach concentrating on the known area of expertise would probably omit questions on any other areas, such as farming, with which the teacher might also be familiar. It is in such a light that anyone interested in conducting an oral history must proceed. A good rule of thumb: Decide what you want to know.

The Interview

Historian William Tyrrell writes: "The first confrontation between questioner and informant represents a duel. The former thrusts to find out how much knowledge the latter has, while the latter parries to determine how much he can trust his interrogator."[9] Although this statement seems more appropriate for a spy novel, it does bring out an important point for oral history. There must be a rapport between the interviewer and the person questioned.

Obviously, certain requirements must be met before any meaningful interview can take place. The first important decision to make is who should be interviewed. The most obvious response is older people because of their many experiences. Certainly older residents should be interviewed, but oral history should not be limited only to their reminiscences. Current leaders can be very helpful in explaining recent events in which they may have played an important role. Some of these events or policies may greatly affect the future of a community. For example, in researching a new volunteer fire department, interview the younger people who organized and established it.

The choice of people to interview depends on the knowledge or information desired. (In our project, the class knew that the township was once the site of a great oil boom and wanted more information on this topic. Several people, hearing of this interest, told students to see a local resident who had once had several very productive wells.) A group of people may also be interviewed, such as the trustees and clerk about the functioning of the local government.

After selecting the individual and obtaining his/her permission, it is then necessary to arrange a suitable time and setting for the interview. Generally, the situation should be one where the interviewee is in familiar surroundings—to make the person feel more comfortable. When asking permission for the interview, give reasons for the request. In addition, give a general description of the kind of information desired. This allows the person time to recollect facts and to assemble any available records. Also, ask permission for students to go along on an interview. Generally, it is a good idea for the teacher to take along two students who are familiar with the person. This tends to relax the interviewee as well as the students. Before going on the interview, discuss with the students exactly what they are to do. Students who go on an interview should be well prepared. All their homework should be done, including practicing the use of interview instruments through role plays.

Certain general guidelines may be helpful when conducting the interviews. Be a good listener and focus attention upon the person. It is important to be sympathetic but noncommittal at the same time. Do not agree or disagree with the facts, simply gather them. At all times try to be congenial yet frank. Make the interviewee feel at ease. Perhaps before beginning, it may be advisable to break the ice by talking about a relevant matter. In addition to these suggestions, use a tape recorder with a built-in microphone. Tape players can inhibit people but this type allows for the greatest disguise.

Finally, considering the age and health of the person interviewed, usually two hours are adequate for discussion. After a certain point, everyone simply becomes tired. As mentioned earlier, the people interviewed will in most cases be extremely cooperative, depending, to a great extent, on how they are approached. The best way is a friendly, honest approach. When I look back upon our eighteen tapes, I am amazed at how very different the people recorded were—some reluctant to discuss certain things, others delighted to tell stories of events or people.

Several more specific points should also be noted during the interview. If a statement is not understood, ask a question again. In doing so, however, don't badger the person or sound like a prosecutor cross-examining a witness. Rephrase the question and use a different manner. Eliminate unclear comments by restating what the person is understood to have said and ask if such a statement is correct. In addition, be time-conscious. To establish a basic chronology, try to get the date of an event. If the person doesn't know, ask if it were before, after, or about the same time as an event he/she knows about. To bring out cause and effect relationships of certain events, ask followup questions like "What was the effect of . . .?" Also, don't be afraid to ask about technical terms. Finally, use simple followup questions such as "How . . .?" and "Why . . .?" These last few points are extremely important. Listening to the first tapes can be useless unless one understands what the person meant. And remember, always, to check the recorder after the first few sentences to be sure it is in fact recording the information.

Another useful suggestion comes from Willa U. Baum:

> Interviewing is one time when a negative approach is more effective than a positive one. Ask about the negative aspects of a situation. For example, in asking about a person, do not begin with a glowing description of him. "I know the mayor was a very generous and wise person. Did you find him so?" Few narrators will quarrel with a statement like that even though they may have found the mayor a disagreeable person. You will get a more lively answer if you start out in the negative. "Despite the mayor's reputation for good works, I hear he was a very difficult man for his immediate employees to get along with." If your narrator admired the mayor greatly, he will spring to his defense with apt illustration of why your statement is wrong. If he did find him hard to get along with, your remark has given him a chance to illustrate some of the mayor's more unpleasant characteristics.[10]

This is not a recommendation to challenge a particular account, but rather to point out that there may be a different version and to give the person a chance to refute it. It is also important not to interrupt a good story with questions that suddenly come to mind. Remember not to be a compulsive talker who allows him/herself to be interviewed. A final word of caution: Do not use the interview to show off personal knowledge, vocabulary, charm.[11]

Upon completion of the interview, be sure to obtain a signed statement granting permission to use the information gained in the interview. (My students had these slips signed after the interviewees had an opportunity to look at the written transcriptions of their tapes.)

Organization after the Interview

After the interview is complete, there are two choices, depending upon the purpose: (1) keep the tape as a record of the interview (but in writing a local history this choice serves no purpose), or (2) transfer the information from the tapes to writing. The latter is an awesome task. With good organization, however, transcription can go very smoothly as a student project. Assign two or three students to do each tape based upon their interest or participation in the interview to be transcribed. Their job is to write down word-for-word everything recorded on the tape. While this could be a very boring task, students usually enjoy doing it. Give each student group a tape player, the original tape, a folder with the name of the person or group interviewed, and a key sheet (see Appendix C).

The key sheet is a numbered list of categories based on the interview sheet. As they transcribe the tapes, students add the information to a page numbered for the appropriate category. For example, if the interviewee talked about the building of a certain church, the information would be written on page #7, headed "Religion." Information on education would be written on page #3, on organizations on page #5, and so on. Thus, when it comes time to compile the information on religion, all that is necessary is to take every page labeled #7, "Religion," from the various folders. When in doubt about a classification—such as whether the story of a blacksmith shop should go under "Early History and Settlement" or "Economic Development"—students should check with the teacher. Most student questions will be of this type. If the entire class makes the arbitrary classifications to begin with, develops the instrument around them, conducts the interviews using them, and then logically transcribes the tapes using them, the students generally will know what information belongs in each category.

After a group of students finishes transcribing a tape, have another group transcribe it as a double check. To finish transcribing all the tapes, students can work on them during class time or study hall, at home, after school, and even on Saturdays.

This stage is an essential part of the research. It should be the most exciting learning experience of all because it is the epitome of student involvement and interest. As one of my students wrote in the final evaluation: ". . . student participation is half the fun of working." The youngster did an excellent job.

Equipment

The equipment my class used consisted of cassette players and tapes. Although lacking the fidelity or durability of reel-to-reel recorders, they proved adequate. They are light and compact. Tapes can be put in or taken out easily without threading problems. Be cautious of the less expensive tapes—they often break after extended use.

Summary

My class's success in doing local history can be attributed to the procedures detailed in the foregoing pages. Similar results are possible for other classes. Teachers have only to see the great enthusiasm generated by undertaking such a project—by its very nature, it is exciting. Students move from the stage of listening to doing, becoming involved in the process of history itself. As the teacher guides them through outlined steps, their enthusiasm and involvement multiply. As the class goes outside the school and involves the community, many other facets enlarge the project, including old photographs, diaries, letters, newspapers, records that the class can get "into." In addition, local projects can have a sort of snowball effect. The more sources the class visits for information, the more the community will talk about the project, and the more contributions the community will make.

Finally, there is the payoff. The class can see its work transformed into something of lasting value. I will never forget my students' faces when I showed them the first printed copy of *The Wilderness That Became Lawrence.*

REFERENCES

1. Donald Dean Parker, *Local History: How to Gather It, Write It, and Publish It* (New York: Social Science Research Council, 1944), p. 65.

2. Thomas E. Felt, *Researching, Writing, and Publishing Local History* (Nashville, Tenn.: American Association for State and Local History, 1976), p. 45.

3. Parker, *Local History*, p. 70.

4. Church Records of the Moss Run United Church of Christ.

5. Felt, *Researching*, p. 20.

6. Parker, *Local History*, p. 20.

7. William G. Tyrrell, "Tape-Recording Local History" (American Association for State and Local History Technical Leaflet 35), *History News* 21, no. 5 (May 1966, rev. 1973).

8. Ibid.

9. Ibid.

10. Willa U. Baum, *Oral History for the Local Historical Society* (Nashville, Tenn.: American Association for State and Local History, 1971), p. 33.

11. Ibid., pp. 32–33.

CHAPTER 4
ORGANIZING AND EVALUATING THE RESEARCH

At some point in the project the teacher must decide when the research is complete. Determining when the class has enough information to begin organizing and writing is not an easy task. Basically, the stopping point will be when the teacher feels the group has exhausted the various sources of information for the topic(s) selected at the beginning of the project. Time may very well be an important factor to consider; various deadlines may have to be met. These factors, along with the scope of the project, will help the teacher decide when to stop researching.

Research Guidelines

At this time the class is ready to take all the information collected and organize it in logical fashion. What may appear an undigested group of facts and materials must be arranged into what will eventually be the finished history. To make this task as easy as possible, students should follow certain guidelines from the very beginning. Most important is proper note-taking from sources. Before either teacher or students take one page of notes, they should be in agreement concerning such details as using the same size paper and copying the facts of reference carefully from each source. This will involve several English lessons in the use of footnotes and bibliographies, style, and similar matters. Such instruction should be a prerequisite to the actual research. Then, when it comes time to prepare footnotes and a bibliography, the necessary facts will be readily available, rather than left to memory.

One way to note information from sources is in small groups. For example, the teacher and a small group of younger students might research various records of proceedings, going through the information carefully, noting those items considered important by the group. Students can record the data in accordance with agreed-upon instructions concerning the use of quotation marks, capitalization, and so forth. Each session of this kind may be very time-consuming and much like a mini-class. However, it will usually end with a great deal of discussion and brainstorming. In my own case, it was necessary to note details in this way with eighth graders who, for the most part, do not have the experience and knowledge to proceed by themselves. With older students, depending upon their ability and experience, a great deal of time may be saved by letting them do the research and note-taking.

The sharing of information can be a very important part of the project because it keeps everyone up-to-date. Students who find certain smaller items (e.g., pages from diaries, descriptions from old books, army discharges) should make copies to share with the rest of the class. When groups complete an article or other activity, they should share it, also. Because different groups will be working with different sources, it is important to assign students to groups researching matters of interest to them. This helps maintain enthusiasm. For example, students who attend a particular church may wish to be assigned to the group that examines the records of the church.

Organizing the Material

At the completion of research and note-taking from any one source, the note sheets should go into the appropriate topical folder—"Government," "Religion," "Economic Development." When all the tapes of the oral history are transcribed, place each sheet containing information on particular topics given by each person in the appropriate folder. (Oral history should probably be done last because by this time students are more knowledgeable about the local area and the interviews tend to be better.) Then, at the end of the research process, each folder will contain all the information on the topic. This system of organization works. Whether all teachers use this particular method is not nearly as important as that they use some logical organization.

Interpreting and Evaluating the Material

Once the information is organized and arranged, it needs to be interpreted and evaluated. The objective is to try to reconstruct the past from the many records and accounts that students have collected. The role of the historian is to make judgments about the past from the information acquired. Unlike science or math, however, more often than not there is no one right answer. Therefore, the historian must make the most logical interpretation from the facts available. Different historians may, of course, interpret information differently. Felt considers three important questions of interest to anyone studying local history which are crucial to the final writing.[1] The first: "How does one choose between conflicting statements in different sources?" This problem can be especially apparent with oral history when one person gives one account and another person gives a varying account of the same incident. Felt's second question: "How does one really prove that something happened the way the best evidence indicates it happened?" And his third question: "How does one deal with the problem of what motivates people to act as they do, and more generally, what causes the events we describe to occur?" These are tough, good questions which should be resolved before writing the history. In the final analysis, they will be answered by the individual's best information, observations, and conclusions.

In evaluating information there are three criteria to consider: *closeness, competence,* and *impartiality*. Any information that satisfies these criteria should receive preference. Closeness refers to "the closest source to the event in time and space, if not an actual observer or participant."[2] For example, there may be two different accounts of the structure and location of the community's first high school, which is no longer standing. One account may come from a man who helped build the school, the other from a person who attended the school at a later date. In terms of closeness, the former account would seem more accurate. If there are conflicting accounts of an event, try to find more information which would verify one version, whenever possible. The second criterion in evaluating information, competence, refers to "the source most capable of understanding and describing a situation."[3] It is based on some sort of expertise in the area of investigation. For example, a teacher in a particular school would be more likely to accurately describe the curriculum of the school than a parent whose child attended it. The third criterion, impartiality, is "the source with the least to gain from a distortion of the record."[4] Felt offers some important advice when considering records and impartiality: look for information in a particular document that it was not intended to give.

The use of these criteria can help immensely in resolving conflicts and supplying the most probable interpretations. In my own class, we went through this information evaluation process as we prepared outlines for the writing of each topic.

When, through this cooperative venture, the class has organized and evaluated the evidence, and made the necessary interpretations and judgments, it is time to start the final stage of the project—writing the history.

REFERENCES

[1] Thomas E. Felt, *Researching, Writing, and Publishing Local History* (Nashville, Tenn.: American Association for State and Local History, 1976), p. 3.

[2] Ibid., pp. 7–9.

[3] Ibid.

[4] Ibid.

CHAPTER 5
WRITING AND PUBLISHING LOCAL HISTORY

After completing the organization of research material, the class is ready for the writing stage. Student notes will serve as the basis for this. No doubt the story will not be as complete as students and teacher might wish, but this is only natural when doing a local history. Everything cannot be included, not only because of evaluation criteria, but also because of space and time limitations. Since all the notes are arranged in topical fashion, go to the folders. The first step is to outline each section, an exercise which is an excellent teaching device as well as an essential requirement for writing a history. Meticulously filter the notes and prepare topical outlines for each section from which to write the text. Writing the text is the most difficult part of the project, particularly for younger children who may not have the expertise or experience to write very well. (This should not be the case for older students.) Even though some of their work may need rewriting by the teacher, students should write the sections—they should not entirely bypass this step! All students need not write, however, only those with the most writing ability. The rest of the class can work on picture selection and captions, illustrations, and the like.

Since this publication is intended as a guide for doing local history projects, I will not devote a great deal of time to writing style. A good style manual such as Turabian's *Manual for Writers*[1] should be used to give the work the necessary consistency. Certainly, the composition should include smooth transitions, clarity, and conciseness of expression. As Felt notes, it is perfectly acceptable to use a similar type work as a model, noting the qualities that appear to make it excellent.[2]

A final word of caution in writing the manuscript: Be willing to rewrite, reorganize, and accept changes suggested by resource people who help edit the final project. Don't be upset the first time a casual observer reads the rough draft of a section and makes several criticisms. Knowing all the months of work that went into the section, one may become defensive. Learn to replace such a reaction with a willingness to listen and change what may need changing. In the end, resource people will help make the final writing a much better product.

Components of the Book

The following sections describe the major parts of the book, in addition to the text.

Title Page

This page gives notice of the title of the work. It can be artistically arranged, yet very simply done. It should not be overcrowded, but should impart to the reader what is in store.

Copyright Notice

This notice serves to protect the work; it appears on the reverse of the title page. It includes the word *Copyright* and/or the letter C within a circle (©), the year of publication, and the name of the person(s) or company claiming the copyright. In our case, the copyright claimant was the entire class.

According to the new copyright law effective January 1, 1978, copyright is secured automatically when the work is created. (The old law required either publication with the copyright notice or registration in the Copyright Office to secure the copyright.) A notice of copyright should still appear in all publicly distributed copies of the work. Registration with the Copyright Office, although not required, also has certain advantages.[3] For more complete information, contact the Copyright Office (Library of Congress, Washington, D.C. 20559).

Preface

This part of the book appears at the beginning, after the title page and copyright notice. It may appear before or after the table of contents. It explains the nature of the work and acknowledges the people who have contributed to it. If it is written by someone other than the author, it is called a *foreword*.

Table of Contents

The guide to what is included in the book and where it may be found, the table of contents lists the title and beginning page number of each major part of the book (i.e., preface, chapters, references).

Footnotes and Bibliography

The purpose of footnotes is to acknowledge the use of material that is not original. While there are various styles of footnotes, the important thing is to be consistent in whatever style is used. Each footnote should be numbered in the text with the source(s) for each one listed at the foot of the page or the end of the chapter (or book). A style manual can provide details concerning the information required. For the local history, I recommend listing footnotes at the end of each chapter.

The bibliography lists the sources used in writing the book—not necessarily every work examined, but those sources found to be most helpful. It is placed at the end of the publication. Here, again, the style manual can provide details concerning the information necessary for each bibliographical entry.

Pictures and Illustrations

The addition of photographs to each chapter can enhance the interest and quality of the local history. Such material should be selected according to quality and appropriateness; however, it should not be added just for the sake of having pictures. Go through a very strenuous selection process to determine which ones to use. Include student illustrations also, with the class selecting the best student works. Student-written captions to accompany both pictures and illustrations can be another class project. Be sure to credit all such materials and to secure written permission for use when necessary.

Preparing the Dummy

Together with the text, the foregoing components are the basic elements of the book. Other parts may be added such as an index at the end or a frontispiece facing the title page. The latter usually consists of a picture or an illustration.

Once the rough draft is complete, the services of several resource people will be helpful—depending on specific needs—to edit the work, to offer technical advice, and to give suggestions for improvement. For example, an English teacher or a writer might edit the rough draft, making grammatical corrections, changing placement of different parts, checking for consistency. Such work is essential and will add greatly to the readability of the final product.

Then it is time to tie everything together—for typists to prepare the final manuscript, for pictures to be cropped and captions typed. After the manuscript has been proofread and all errors found and corrected, it is time to go to the printer.

Selecting a Printer

Since the work is primarily of local interest, there is little chance of finding a professional publisher. This is to be expected. Aside from the question of finances, it is very helpful to know what services a competent printer can provide. Prior to completion of the manuscript, it is a good idea to talk to several local printers about publication before choosing one because this decision is a very important one. Factors to consider might include the company's experience in printing local works, enthusiasm or interest in the local history, and, of course, price.

In discussions with one or more printers, one can learn about options for composition, paper, and binding. It would be advisable to get prices for each option. For example, a book set in type can add several hundred dollars to the cost. An alternative would be to provide typewritten copy ready for photographing. Similarly, various papers can also affect the price. Thus, budgetary restrictions may determine the selection. The binding price can also be a large variable in cost. A book of 96 pages could be saddle stitched, perfect bound with paper covers, or case bound with stiff cloth covers.

The printer can provide more complete details and alternatives concerning these and other decisions to be made. It is evident, then, that the printer plays an extremely valuable role in the appearance of the final product.

Financing the Project

Several sources may be approached for the financing of the project. First of all, there are the local civic groups such as the Lions Club or the Kiwanis Club. Other groups that might help defray expenses are historical societies, churches, and fraternal orders. Probably the most appropriate group to approach would be the local parent-teacher organization. The amount of money required for such a project will depend upon the printing decisions, the people employed to help, the fees charged by organizations, and similar expenses. In the end, however, the project should pay for itself in sales. In fact, a profit should be realized.

Up to publication expenses should consist of buying cassette tapes, paying the typists, and a considerable amount of local travel. While not an overwhelming burden to bear, these costs can be financed by various class moneymaking projects. The real expense comes with actual publication of the book. Possibly, the local printers may agree to let the payment ride until sales are made. However, financial profit should not be a major consideration in undertaking this project. Indeed, such a reward would be small when compared to the many learning situations encountered.

Once the book goes to the printer, there are several basic economic decisions to make: (1) How many copies should be published? (2) How should the book be advertised and marketed? (3) What price should be charged for the book? The answers to these questions can come through class discussions. As for the number of copies for the initial publication, this figure will be based upon the estimated number of readers to be reached. The size of the local population will be the biggest determinant in arriving at this decision. The greatest advertising will probably be through word of mouth. The local newspaper may, however, do a special article about the project, reaching almost everyone in the area. As for marketing, the book may be sold at school and at local stores within the community. With respect to price, the printer can provide different cost breakdowns depending upon the number of copies to be published. Discuss with the class the various expenses and "break-even point." Obviously, some sort of profit will be possible. After considering such factors, teacher and students can arrive at a price for the book. There are no hard rules for determining answers to these questions; the answers depend upon an evaluation of the local circumstances.

Finally, the big day comes when the books are delivered to the school. In my own case, I was hard pressed to find words to aptly describe my personal feelings and those of my students. The most gratifying part probably came later on hearing such comments from the community as "I didn't know that happened here," or "That sure was interesting about . . . ." Indeed, the satisfaction experienced by both teacher and students is well earned and deserved.

REFERENCES

1. Kate L. Turabian, *A Manual for Writers* (Chicago: University of Chicago Press, 1973).
2. Thomas E. Felt, *Researching, Writing, and Publishing Local History* (Nashville, Tenn.: American Association for State and Local History, 1976), p. 69.
3. Circular R1, *Copyright Basics,* and Circular R99, *Highlights of the New Copyright Law* (Washington, D.C.: Copyright Office, Library of Congress, September 1980 and January 1979).

CHAPTER 6
STUDENT PARTICIPATION

We should be concerned with the instructional efficiency of a given history as much as we are concerned with overall significance of any given history. History teachers must give attention to this issue or watch the further demise of history in schools.[1]

The purpose in carrying out the local project is to "do history." As evidenced in many classrooms across the nation, the study of history tends not to be the most popular subject. Instead, more often than not, it is the seemingly endless digestion and regurgitation of facts with no apparent justification. By "doing history," however, participation and self-discovery bring home to students the value of the subject. In fact, the project puts life into history.

Most teachers today would agree that one of their most difficult problems is motivating students. But when students are properly motivated, the most exciting kind of learning results. Local history projects can provide such motivation, because students can readily identify with the local community. My own goal as a teacher has always been to provide instructional material in such a manner that students learn from it. For me, this means presenting the material in the most enjoyable fashion possible. Simultaneous learning and enjoyment need not be mutually exclusive. A local history project can provide both.

Once student interest and motivation are gained by beginning the project, they must be maintained. Teachers can accomplish this by constantly encouraging class participation in the entire process. It is the students' project, and they must be allowed to make decisions about every aspect of it. Given this responsibility, students will fulfill the necessary expectations. The teacher's role is that of guide, research helper, and maintainer of interest. The degree of teacher activity depends partly upon the age level and ability of the class. The wide variety of topics to be covered encompass every subject area of the curriculum, and the only limitations are imagination and creativity.

As noted at the outset of this guide, the initial task is to select a topic—the first decision the class will have to make. Because classroom discussions are an indispensable part of the whole process, brainstorming is an often-used technique. After deciding upon the area of inquiry, the class is ready to do the research.

Research investigation should involve everyone. Related activities include reading, note-taking, interpreting materials, finding information, making field trips, using the library, taking and collecting photographs, interviewing people, and decisionmaking. The class learns the methodology of history by doing it. Teacher and student should decide the role of each participant, trying, as much as possible, to link individual interests with talents. For example, an excellent reader who is extremely interested in a particular historical event may readily agree to read and note written materials about the event. Another student who loves photography might become a photographer. A third student who has good listening skills can be invaluable in helping groups transcribe tapes.

Upon completion of class research, it is time to begin organizing the material for writing. This is a time for exciting discussions to determine the validity of often-conflicting accounts of events. Related skills needed in this process include outlining, writing, footnoting, art work, layouts, design, preparing a bibliography, and, again, decisionmaking—all of which are part of the curriculum. The difference between carrying out these activities and just doing similar exercises is that the activities are leading toward a goal—they have a purpose that students can see and will work to attain.

Then, when the manuscript nears publication, it is time to make business decisions and to be sure that certain technicalities and legalities such as permissions have been obtained. Related activities include typing, final layout, financing, pricing, marketing, and distribution. Enthusiasm will be at a peak as students are about to see the results of their efforts. Very likely it may be possible to see that the project has had quite a maturing effect upon the learners. Indeed, they have "done history."

With publication, the local history project is by no means complete. Innumerable, but meaningful, followup activities based upon the work may be carried out. For example, my class wrote a three-act play about a dramatic episode in our history and presented it to the community. The next year, another class used the local history to make many outstanding slide-tape presentations of the past. Thus, what may seem an end can be only a beginning for additional interesting history activities. Perhaps some comments from the class that wrote our book can best exemplify these effects. A few days before final publication of the book, students wrote an essay about the entire project, including what they liked, disliked, felt they had learned from the project. Among the typical comments were the following:

- —"The interviews were always interesting and fun. We learned something new each time."
- —"Even though a certain area is very small it still can become a very important part of someone's life."
- —"To me this is the greatest experience I have ever had."
- —"In writing this book all the kids in our class participated. One of the things I liked best is I know more now about Lawrence Township than before."

Student-teachers constantly ask supervising teachers and others, "What can I do with the class?" Classroom teachers still seek new answers to this question. It is hoped that this guide answers it in a way that will bring to other classes the same exciting reward it has brought to my students, namely, enthusiasm, motivation, excitement, and most importantly—learning.

REFERENCE

[1] Richard R. Newton, "Oral History: Using the School as a Historical Institution," *Clearing House* 48 (October 1973): 78.

CHAPTER 7
LOCAL HISTORY ACTIVITIES

In addition to the many opportunities for student involvement during the course of the local history project, numerous followup activities can be beneficial learning experiences—some during the course of the project, others upon its completion.

Slide-Tape Presentations

An increasingly popular form of communication and orientation, this technique challenges student imagination and creativity. Students may prepare slide-tape presentations from information gained in the local history, choosing from a wide range of subjects. Basically, the technique requires slides—taken with cameras or made from existing pictures—and an audio presentation. Since making slides from previously taken pictures can be expensive, it is a good idea to go to a media center which has an ektagraphic visualmaker that makes slides from original pictures. Once the slides are available, it is time to write the script. Often music may accompany the taped narration, but the combination of these ingredients is the decision of the students.

When they have completed the slide-tape, students may present it to civic groups (as several of my students did with amazing success) or enter it as a project in local and regional history fairs. In any event, the final product may be a means of sharing the local historical experience with others. A Portland, Oregon, teacher and a group of eighth graders shared their slide-tape show of historical landmarks with third graders, followed by a field trip in which the third graders, accompanied by the eighth graders, visited the historical landmarks.[1] These are just a few of the many uses and variations of the local slide-tape presentation.

Archaeological Digs

This activity might well be part of the research process. Artifacts found during the course of the research can often be of historical significance because they can help explain community life at a given time period. An excellent method of teaching the role of archaeology in history is to participate in it in some fashion. Student participation in such activities should of course be preceded by a careful briefing on the historic value and irreplaceable nature of these materials. It may be possible to arrange for an archaeologist from a local college or university to give a lecture on the topic and also accompany the class to a site. Excited students have visited local sites to look for artifacts and make deductions from them. A Hamilton, Massachusetts, teacher, for instance, had his sixth graders dig in cellars built before the Revolutionary War. (Early maps they had discovered guided them to the cellars.) Equipped with the necessary gear, they uncovered more than fifty bits of artifacts including pottery, china, animal bones, and teeth. As one student described the experience, "It was thrilling to handle pieces of dishes and bottles used by people who had lived during the French and Indian War, the Constitutional Convention, Thomas Jefferson's purchase of Louisiana, and John Marshall's historic Supreme Court sessions."[2]

Dramatics

Dramatics can include writing and presenting a local history play, preparing a historical pageant, or devising a program for radio. The class may choose a particularly dramatic episode from the local history and spend several weeks writing the script, reconstructing the event in the best manner possible from the available evidence. Because of the localized nature of the work, the community will enjoy sharing with students a part of the community's past. Students may also produce other well-organized activities along these lines.

Genealogy

The great popularity of the television program and book, *Roots,* has directed many people to the study of their ancestry—an activity students and parents can share. Nothing seems to excite people more about history than searching for their own roots. At the beginning of the project, students may begin tracing their family trees. In doing so, they will not only learn a great deal about who they are, but they will come across many papers and records that will add to the entire local history. When studying United States history, my students found it interesting to discover which of their forebears lived during that time period. One student won first place in a state regional history fair with her genealogical event.

Visiting Cemeteries

Local cemeteries can be an excellent source for uncovering history. While they may not appear initially desirable as a field trip site, they can be very revealing and worthwhile. War markers are a source of both information and discussion about various wars. Epitaphs can be especially revealing to students, so that their visits can aid them in tracing family trees. History can indeed be read from tombstones.

Communicative Education

While this term has various definitions and connotations, it generally refers to oral activities in which one obtains information about a community from its citizenry. Certainly the oral history fits this description. The *Foxfire* books are another excellent example of what can be done from such activities. The journalism class that prepared these books found information on a number of topics, ranging from making banjos to building log cabins to telling ghost stories. In carrying out such tasks, students learn to communicate effectively with people usually not in their age group. From talking to people with dissimilar attitudes and positions, they begin to understand how communicative barriers may develop. After our oral history was complete, students looked at elderly people in a much different light.

Communication activities employ more instructional strategies than any single subject area of the curriculum. The class of a junior college teacher in Oklahoma investigating local history, for example, found stories of huge oil booms and tales of outlaws. After interviewing older citizens about their knowledge of these events, students gave oral reports in class.[3] To carry out the assignment, students had to do research, use proper interview techniques, communicate effectively, transcribe information, and give a good oral presentation of their work. Activities of this nature are especially motivational and interesting to learners.

History Fairs

Only in recent years have history fairs been recognized and conducted. They are an excellent way to share with the community student work in history. A fair may be limited to projects of local nature or broadened to include all United States history. Whatever the emphasis, students can prepare appropriate skits, dioramas, or models; or demonstrate folk dancing of the period. Other activities or projects include slide-tape shows, plays, pageants, songs. A variation is a folk fair.

> The purpose of the Folk Fair is to acquaint the people of the community (and the rest of the student body) with the customs, foods, products, and costumes of various nationality groups whose descendants are represented in the community, and thus to lead to further understanding of the community's heritage.[4]

Another project along these lines is a "Pioneer Day," a day when residents dress as pioneers and conduct classes, demonstrating to students such early crafts as churning butter, trapping, shooting muzzleloaders. Any of these activities will enhance community interest, as well as share knowledge of local interest. A final idea is an heirloom show in which parents and students bring in family heirlooms such as letters, tools, kitchen implements, old spectacles—anything with a story. Students then identify the object, describing its use and its role in the family history.[5]

Bulletin Boards

Bulletin boards are an excellent device for sharing interesting material of a local nature. For example, a class might "construct a bulletin board displaying five enlarged photographs of old buildings in the community. Place the date of each building's completion above its picture. Below each, have children indicate what events of national importance took place during that particular period."[6] Or "personify the county courthouse or the town's municipal building and have it explain changes in the community that have taken place since it was built. Have it include modes of travel, industry in the area, increase or decrease of population, schools, or any aspect of community life familiar to the children."[7] An eighth grader who took photographs of every road in her township (about twenty-five) made an imaginative bulletin board display entitled "All Roads Lead Home." She included a moving essay about the community's past and the pride she had for her community. Obviously, students can create an infinite number and variety of displays, all based on the sharing of local history in some way.

Historical Geography

Inherent in the study of local history is the significant role geography played in the community's settlement and development. Have the class make maps, because students find it fun to make deductions based upon their interpretation of maps. Thus besides increasing their map skills, students will be carrying out an essential part of any local historian's investigation. Apparent questions they can answer from this activity include the following:

1. What might be the geographical reason for the community's settlement at certain sites?
2. Do certain ethnic groups dominate any particular areas?
3. If so, why?
4. What were some routes of early immigration and emigration?

The answers to questions of this type will demonstrate the important link between history and geography.

Time Capsules

Burying time capsules became a very popular Bicentennial event. However, it need not be an exercise limited to every one or two hundred years! Whenever it is carried out, this activity can stir up a great deal of interest as well as provide future generations with an excellent source of historical data. An industrial supply company may donate a large fiberglass capsule. Include in the capsule many remnants of the past collected while doing the local history, as well as certain items of a contemporary nature. An excellent perspective to take in preparing materials is to determine what people of the future would want to know about the people of today. This should lead naturally to a real examination of present-day culture and the inclusion of many photographs of the contemporary community, as well as samples of popular fashions, fads, songs, sports. Also add to the capsule the original oral cassette tapes, several of the local history books, and old papers. These are just a few of the endless varieties of materials to study and prepare to bury.

Junior Historical Society

The knowledge gained from some of the previously mentioned activities can logically lead to an interest in or the creation of a junior historical society. The state or area may well have some such groups. If so, it may be very worthwhile to look into them. If not, this may be an excellent opportunity for the teacher to lead and guide student interest in history. Too often this type of organization is not started because of a general misconception that teenagers are not interested in history. This simply is not true. The creation of such a group can prove it. Students should be involved from the beginning. For example, they should structure a constitution providing the basic government of the organization for conducting its activities. Ultimately, the success or failure of the group, to a large extent, depends upon the sponsor, whose role is to help maintain the enthusiasm of the members.

Some activities of the junior historical society might include an awards program, a newsletter, projects involving historical field work, and tours to historical sites.[8] In addition, any of the activities described earlier are appropriate for such a group.

Field Trips

Often, class-sponsored field trips overlook rich possibilities right at home. To do so is to bypass some very interesting and informative historical sites. Often, too, the sites selected for visitation are those associated with national events. This is not to say that such places are unimportant, but to point out that local places can be just as interesting, exciting, and significant. For example, in doing our local history, we took small-group field trips to cemeteries, caves, old coal mines, even several area homes. In fact, one woman's home was a minimuseum containing antiques of a varied nature collected over the years. This local resident spent many enjoyable afternoons giving the "grand tour" to students. Thus student field trips to local historical sites can be excellent learning experiences.

These are just a few of the many local history activities that are available for student participation. Their purpose is the same as the actual writing of the local history—to teach history by doing it. By encouraging student involvement in this manner, the teacher will not only create and sustain their interest in history, but will provide pupils with some of the most meaningful educational experiences they have ever had.

REFERENCES

1. J. T. Leeson, "Focusing on the Local Scene," *Instructor* 82 (April 1972): 136–37.
2. William Heitz, "Digging Up Local History," *Instructor* 83 (April 1974): 46–47.
3. David L. Serres, "Black Gold and Wildcats," *Communication Education* 25 (September 1966): 255–58.
4. Clifford L. Lord, *Teaching History with Community Resources* (New York: Columbia University, Teachers College Press, 1964).
5. Ibid., p. 70.
6. William Smith, "History—Something We Read About in Books," *Instructor* 81 (October 1971): 140.
7. Ibid.
8. Robert W. Montgomery, "History for Young People: Organizing a Junior Society" (American Association for State and Local History Technical Leaflet 44), *History News* 22, no. 9 (September 1967, rev. 1972).

APPENDIX A
*OUTLINE FOR RESEARCHING AND WRITING LOCAL HISTORY**

I. Geography and Topography
    A. Physical characteristics of the area
    B. Natural resources—mines, forest, fisheries, etc.
    C. Soil—its kind and quality
    D. Climate

II. Antiquities—Indians
    A. Indian mounds, rock carvings, copper and stone implements
    B. Indian life and civilization
    C. Indian-white relationships
    D. Indian treaties and removal of Indians from the area

III. Pioneer Settlement
    A. Conditions which made the area desirable as a home
        Indians—absent or still present when settlement began
        Land—wooded or prairie
        Transportation—difficult or relatively easy
        Sources of Income—immediate or to be developed
        Markets—nearby or far away
    B. Character and composition of the early settlers
        Nationality by birth and parentage—native American or immigrants
        Home of settlers immediately preceding their coming
        Route followed from the old to the new home
        Motives which led to their coming
        Old-home occupations of settlers compared with the new-home activities
        Special characteristics of the early settlers

---

* From *Local History: How to Gather It, Write It, and Publish It* by Donald Dean Parker. Copyright © 1944 by the Social Science Research Council. Reprinted with permission.

Relations between different racial or national groups, e.g., whites and Negroes; French, Germans, and British, etc.
  C. Biographical sketches of outstanding pioneers
     The "founders"
     Their chief supporters and advisors
  D. Map of the area shortly after settlement
     Explanation of details and matters not readily apparent

IV. Economic Developments
   A. Transportation, trade, and communications:
      General relations to other communities, sections, countries
      General nature of trade, in relation to agriculture, manufacturing, etc.
      Frontier trade—furs, etc.
      Roads, rivers, and canals
      Maritime trade
      Railroads
      Telegraph and telephone
      The automobile
      Air routes
      Mail services
   B. Agriculture:
      General ideals and methods
      Subsistence farming
      Lumbering and forestry
      Money crops—their relation to trade
      Machinery and implements
      Rotation and fertilization
      Animal husbandry
      Capital—owning, mortgages, renting, share-cropping, etc.
   C. Manufacturing:
      Early handicrafts
      Inventions and machinery
      The factory system
      Private business and corporations
      Banking and finance
      Labor and the unions

General business relations
D. Maritime activities:
Fisheries
Shipbuilding
E. Extractive industries
Mining, oil, etc. (Lumbering might also be considered under this heading, if the forests were simply cut down without any reforesting.)

V. Political Activities
A. Original form of local government
B. Changes in characters, boundaries, status, etc.
C. Prominent officials
D. Rise and progress of political parties, their local programs, elections, etc.
E. Degree of efficiency and honesty in local government, financial policies, etc.
F. Relation of government to other institutions (churches, schools), social problems, etc.
G. Civic services:
Water
Sewerage
Gas and electricity
Fire and police protection
Public recreation facilities
"City planning"
H. Civic reform movements

VI. Religious Developments
A. Early religious life
B. Development of the major denominations (doctrines, government, ritual, morals)
C. Minor groups
D. Interdenominational relations
E. Moral attitudes in churches, and their relations to social problems, law and order, civic reform, etc.

VII. Population History
A. Birth and death rate
B. Growth or decline of total population
C. Migrations

Immigration:
  Statistics
  Racial or national groups
  Treatment of immigrants
  "Americanization"
  Influence of immigrants
Emigration:
  Causes and destinations
  Selective influences
  Results

VIII. The Family
  A. Courtship, marriage, remarriage, and divorce
  B. Moral standards
  C. Personal and property rights of husbands, wives, and children
  D. Birth rates, and status of children
  E. Special phases of family life—religious, educational, recreational, economic, etc.

IX. Education
  A. The first schools
  B. Church and other private schools
  C. Public schools:
    Elementary and secondary
    Curriculum; and extracurricular activities
    Teachers and teacher training
    Methods of teaching
    School financing
    School building and facilities
    Special schools
  D. Higher education:
    Church colleges
    City or state universities
  E. Adult education
  F. General influence of schools on the community, and vice versa

X. Newspapers, Periodicals, and Libraries
  A. The early newspapers, their origin, growth, and influence

        Political affiliations and part played in local politics
    B. Discontinued newspapers, origin, and influence
        Political affiliations
        Reasons for discontinuance, merging, etc.
    C. The present newspapers, origin, growth, and influence
        Political affiliations
        Their policies for the local community
    D. Periodicals, magazines, and journals
        Origin, growth, influence
    E. Location of the files of present and defunct publications
    F. Libraries—private and public

XI. Social and Fraternal Organizations
    A. Origin and growth of each
    B. Purpose and special field of activity
    C. Relation to whole community

XII. Other Cultural Activities: The Arts
    A. Household arts—cookery, wines, textiles, etc.
    B. Minor arts—costumes, furniture, silver, glass, pottery, embroidery
    C. Fine arts:
        Music—folk songs, singing societies, orchestras, etc.
        Dancing
        Painting and sculpture
        Architecture—old houses, construction, architectural styles, etc.
    D. Literature:
        Taste in reading—relation to libraries, periodicals, etc.
        Literary societies
        Original work
    E. Professional groups and schools (musicians, architects, etc.)
    F. The Stage:
        Amateur theatricals
        Pageants
        Theaters; vaudeville
        Minstrel shows
        "Movies"
        Opera

XIII. Science and Technology
  A. Local inventors
  B. Technological developments in factories, transportation, agriculture, etc.
  C. Original work in "pure science"
  D. Scientific institutions and professional groups (engineers, chemists, etc.)

XIV. Law
  A. Civil law
     Common law—civil
     Statute law (local, state, and federal)
  B. Criminal law
  C. Court organization and procedures
  D. The legal profession—training, place in community, in politics

XV. Social Problems and Reform
  A. Poverty and poor relief
  B. Crime and punishment
     Crime conditions, and moral attitudes
     Types of punishment
     Penology and institutions
  C. Drunkenness and drug addiction
  D. Prostitution
  E. Slavery (a topic needing detailed treatment in the South)
  F. Handicapped classes
     Orphans and aged
     The insane and feebleminded
     The deaf, dumb, blind, and crippled
  G. Health and disease
     Medicine and doctors
     Disease conditions
        Endemic
        Epidemic
     Public health control
     Folk medicine and practice
     Quackery and medical sects
     Relations to regular medicine
     Public medical services

H. Social reform movements

Antislavery, temperance, women's rights, etc. (each of these can be treated in relation to a particular problem above)

XVI. Recreation
A. Utilitarian recreation—corn huskings, house raisings, spelling bees, etc.
B. Indoor games
C. Outdoor sports—amateur and professional
D. (See also literature, libraries, theaters, movies, radio, etc.)
E. Vacations—public "resorts," "amusement parks"
F. Immigrant contributions

XVII. Folklore
A. Superstitions of various sorts
B. Local beliefs about births, deaths, weddings, and funerals
C. Ghosts, charms, haunted houses, hidden stairways, secret closets
D. Strange and unaccounted-for happenings
E. Eccentric characters—inventors, cranks, prophets, gamblers, murderers, spies
F. Spite fences, churches, schools, towns, and railroads
G. Odd decisions made by the flipping of a coin, etc.
H. Irreverent, odd, and interesting jingles on tombstones
I. Odd and obsolete punishments, ordinances, etc.
J. Local sayings, maxims, proverbs, and ballads
K. Dialect and words peculiar to the neighborhood
L. Local sports, feasts, fairs, etc.

APPENDIX B
INTERVIEW SHEET

Name _____ Date _____

    I. Family History
       A. Parents
       B. Earlier Ancestors

   II. Preteen and Adolescence
       A. Work
       B. Recreation
       C. Clothes
       D. Transportation
       E. Money
       F. Hobbies
       G. Food
       H. Living Conditions (water, sewage, refrigeration, heat, light, housing)

  III. Education
       A. Schools
       B. Curriculum
       C. Teachers
       D. Extracurricular Activities
       E. Problems
       F. Money
       G. Discipline
       H. Difference Today

  IV. Religion
       A. Churches
       B. Clergy
       C. Activities

   V. Organizations
       A. Types
       B. Association with (location, purpose)

VI. Occupation
   A. Salary
   B. Employer, Employees
   C. Relative to Lawrence

VII. Civic Involvement
   A. Types

VIII. Methods of Doing Things (Farming, etc.)

IX. Admired People of Lawrence

X. Folklore
   A. Stories Passed Down
   B. Superstitions
   C. Name Derivations
   D. Ghost Stories

XI. Unusual Circumstances
   A. Natural Disasters (floods, fires, tornadoes)
   B. Crime/Scandals
   C. Tragedies

XII. Customs (Dating, Celebrations, Bellowing)

XIII. Photographs, Materials

XIV. Final Comments

APPENDIX C
KEY SHEET
FOR TRANSCRIBING ORAL TAPES

Arrange all the information into one of the following categories:

1. Government
2. Contemporary Community
3. Education
4. Early History and Settlement
5. Organizations
6. Economic Development
7. Religion
8. Geography
9. Folklore
10. Personalities
11. Miscellaneous
12. Customs
13. Unusual Circumstances

Be as accurate as possible.
When in doubt, ask.
Be neat.
Use quotation marks when necessary.

RECOMMENDED READINGS

Bassett, Ruth. "Reading History from Tombstones." *Instructor* (April 1971): 94–96.

Baum, Willa K. *Oral History for the Local Historical Society.* Nashville, Tenn.: American Association for State and Local History by special arrangement with The Conference of California Historical Societies, 1971.

Campbell, William Giles, and Ballou, Stephen Vaughan. *Form and Style Theses, Reports, Term Papers.* Boston: Houghton Mifflin Co., 1974.

Clark, Thomas B. "Local History in a World of Change." Clarence M. Burton Memorial Lecture, Historical Society of Michigan, delivered September 23, 1967.

Cordier, Ralph. "The Study of History Through State and Local Resource," *Social Studies* 60 (March 1969): 99–104

Cumming, John. *A Guide for the Writing of Local History.* Michigan American Revolution Bicentennial Commission, 1974.

Decker, Max J. "Local Folklore: An Untapped Treasure." *School and Community* 59 (October 1972): 23–44.

Felt, Thomas E. *Researching, Writing, and Publishing Local History.* Nashville, Tenn.: American Association for State and Local History, 1976.

Heitz, William. "Digging Up Local History." *Instructor* 83 (April 1974): 46–47.

Hovenier, Peter J., and Krusic, Mary Lou. "Classroom Investigation of the Origin and Historical Geography of Local Communities." *Journal of Geography* 68 (May 1969): 289–94.

Insel, Deborah. "Foxfire in the City." *English Journal* 64 (September 1975): 36–38.

Leeson, J. T. "Focusing on the Local Scene." *Instructor* 82 (April 1972): 136–37.

Leuvan, Daniel Van. "Local History Aids the Teaching of American History." *Social Studies* 62 (November 1971): 247–48.

Lord, Clifford L. *Teaching History with Community Resources.* New York: Columbia University, Teachers College Press, 1964.

Manella, Joseph R. "Dig-In Excites Social Studies." *Education Digest* 37 (April 1972): 32–33.

Montgomery, Robert W. "History for Young People: Organizing a Junior Society." *History News* 22, no. 9 (September 1967).

Neuenschwander, John A. *Oral History as a Teaching Approach.* Washington, D.C.: National Education Association, 1976.

Newton, Richard F. "Oral History: Using the School as a Historical Institution." *Clearing House* 48 (October 1973): 73–78.

Parker, Donald Dean. *Local History: How to Gather It, Write It, and Publish It.* New York: Social Science Research Council, 1944.

Serres, David L. "Black Gold and Wildcats." *Communication Education* 25 (September 1966):255–58.

Smith, William. "History—Something We Read About in Books." *Instructor* 81 (October 1971): 140.

Turabian, Kate L. *A Manual for Writers of Term Papers, Theses, and Dissertations.* Chicago: University of Chicago Press, 1973.

Tyrrell, William G. "Tape-Recording Local History." *History News* 21, no. 5 (May 1966).

Weisenburger, Francis P. *Ohio: A Student's Guide to Localized History.* New York: Columbia University, Teachers College Press, 1965.